EUROPA'S FLIGHT

EUROPA'S FLIGHT
JOHN GREENING

NEW WALK EDITIONS
Leicester • Nottingham

Published by New Walk Editions
c/o Rory Waterman,
Nottingham Creative Writing Hub,
Department of English, Philosophy and Communication,
Nottingham Trent University, NG11 8NS
and
c/o Nick Everett, Centre for New Writing,
University of Leicester, LE1 7RH
www.newwalkmagazine.com

ISBN: 978-1-9998026-8-4

Printed by imprintdigital, Upton Pyne, Exeter.

CONTENTS

Introduction

Europa's Flight is in some ways a sequel to another 'crown of sonnets' (sometimes called Hungarian sonnets) which I wrote exactly twenty years earlier and included in *Hunts: Poems 1979-2009*. 'European Union' presented fourteen nations in fourteen linked sonnets, united by the fifteenth – 'United Kingdom'. But my twenty-first century sequence is a much more dream-like composition. It emerged unbidden from a mood of unease and led me into areas I really wasn't expecting, may not even have liked, but which came to feel important.

The key or clue is in Knossos, which was the main object of our 2017 holiday: Sir Arthur Evans's excavations, the bull-dancers and child sacrifices, Minos, Ariadne, Daedalus (his labyrinth, but also those wax wings for Icarus, the weird wooden cow for Pasiphaë, and a gigantic bronze automaton designed as a weapon of mass destruction). Then, of course, there was the story of Europa's abduction by Zeus. As I wrote, obsessively, unstoppably, the form itself driving me on, autobiography and cultural history began to creep in, tiny details from our holiday (the man who cleaned the swimming pool, a stunned swallow in the villa) and even – Louis MacNeice would have approved – items of news. Brexit is a vital thread running through this verse labyrinth, but the European refugee crisis is there too: it was especially evident in Crete. If I was disconcerted by the direction the poem took, I also knew what Stravinsky had said about *The Rite of Spring*, how he felt he was 'the vessel through which *Le Sacre* passed'.

In a characteristic punning synchronicity, *Europa's Flight* was begun on a plane, and ends beneath one: the tree where Zeus deposited his victim. I wrote about this in an essay on poetry and coincidence for the Royal Literary Fund, explaining that during our stay in Crete I had wanted to visit the tree but decided it was too far north:

> On our last day, we headed instead to the beach at Matala, not knowing it was associated with Joni Mitchell's 'Carey', Jane's

favourite, a song we used to listen to together. That was coincidence enough, but on the way there our taxi driver suddenly pulled over at an archaeological site, Gortyna (or Gortys), and said he would take a smoke while we looked around. It wasn't anywhere we'd planned to come. But inside, beyond the Odeion and the sixth-century engraved Laws of Gortyna, to my astonishment, I found the very thing I had most wanted to see, that I had mistakenly believed to be out of reach: the evergreen plane tree of Europa.

Oh you're a mean old Daddy

Joni Mitchell

1

Europa on his back, he flies to Crete,
escapes that constant croaking, mocking noise
across the Channel. Remember how his feet
once danced a line so Greek she'd even praise
its natural timing? That was Europa's year,
the year they met and got together, on
the hippie fringe of things. But now it's where
slowly a myth has begun to come unspun,
a silken con-trail. The cabin crew intone
emergency procedures. The captain gives
a jaunty commentary from his unseen throne
up in the cockpit where the gods must live,
among the sunny curls and advancing fronts,
since gods can do whatever god-lust wants.

2

Since gods can, do whatever god-lust wants...
the ageing stars sing out from Matala,
and there beneath a plane in Gortys once
Europa's last gasp was the start of mortal
bafflement. We have come to find the maze
Sir Arthur Evans laid for left-hand driving
in a right-hand world. Despite our satnav, phrase-
book apps and fake-news tan, we keep arriving
at the same old Blue. A bull-faced minister
is crouched in Brussels with his nemesis
and doesn't know what's hidden in that stare:
a stone that Zeus's mother swaddled, kissed
and gave to Chronos, which he snatched and ate.
She had no power, she only had her fate.

3

She has no power, she only has her fate,
the Cretan cleaning woman who looked on
as we left Cambridgeshire, passing the gate
where three old yews were this weekend cut down
to make a Mediterranean-style home,
all pines and palms. She would not know our yew
or how it longs to reach a catacomb,
its roots as old as Ariadne's new
and sparkling dance floor, the flutes in its bole
as deeply etched as youth was in the girl
who smiled and said I'm going to leap that bull...
But this is England now, she knows, unfurling
the Dyson Animal. A swing's been planted
and children come, yet still her mind is haunted.

4

The children come, yet still her mind is haunted
by what they have to face each year, fourteen
who've grown up to the challenge, being counted
and waved towards the cave mouth. Touching scene
as parents kiss them off, half proud, still hoping
for some shame-faced reprieve, the crowd on edge
with the thrill of it, unseemly, unstopping,
the chant for blood, for something customs urge
which is by any other standards brutal,
immoral... Condemning it, we soon join in
the countdown from fourteen to none, the fatal
unspooling of a legend set to respin
the world and its polarity to a story,
a labyrinth, a distant stifled roar.

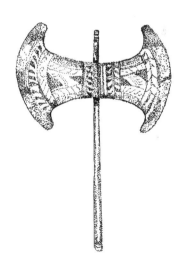

5

A labyrinth, a distant stifled roar,
becomes a screaming British Airways flight,
Daedalus's shade at the cabin door
enquiring if his son was here tonight
with Helios. No answer. The brass declare:
look out, you'll notice that we're passing Samos
and the Icarian Sea... Glissandi veer
from past to present. Down the aisle those nameless
high achievers tread a steady line, ghosts
who lost their way in Caesar's fire, each poet
believing in the piece they clutch. It costs
a lifetime, yet the crafty who follow it
will find there is a heart. Pull down the blinds.
Love, they cry, to laughter. A thread unwinds.

6

Love, we cry, to laughter. A thread unwinds
and leads us back to Knossos, where they build
a new machine for probing ancient minds –
and here it is. Solar-powered, of course, a wild
imaginative leap with Daedalus
that brings us to his presence almost, old
intelligence of Minos's, for us
the source of what's to come. He says: be bold,
my son, aim where the line of your desire
dictates you go. You are in the clutch
of Crete's black widow. If you must aspire
to death by worldly web or at the rich
pulse where creative force makes love to power,
you've read the myths at Pasiphaë's door.

7

You've read the myths. At Pasiphaë's door
the inventor waits. He has his latest thing,
a box shaped like a cow (contrived to lure
in cunning bovine ways) for her little fling
with bull power. He does what she requests,
perverse or weird, he doesn't ask, he makes
and goes on making, but knows this is a test
of indefatigability: a sex-
machine (by royal appointment) to fire
a bull's seed in the Queen's womb. Very nice
for her, and him no doubt, but such desire
could bring down kingly wrath. Too high a price
for Daedalus & Son. They know their friends.
An upright, bronzed, robotic figure stands.

8

An upright, bronze, robotic figure stands
prepared to grasp futurity. A.I.
we'd call it now. It carries in clawed hands
the vellum scrolls, and with its blinking eye
begins reciting. The epic starts in Crete
in wartime, battles, affairs, so many tales –
how those who fought the north wind faced defeat
but found a way through to the promised isles
the other side of Europe. A verse machine,
a line spinner, this mythical creation
creates new myths to fill the old, whose meaning
decays across a cloudless airy ocean
of rhetoric. What next, you frequent flier
with one vein, Daedalus's secret wire?

9

With one vein, Daedalus's secret wire
amuses the crowd – until his oiled parade
stops working. Someone sets the volume higher
but nothing comes. We clutch our phones, afraid
we've lost our playlists, all but these cicadas,
an owlet, a scarab in the swimming pool,
and stars that start to glint and constellate.
The offline night begins. Some hours of cool
before the creature can again be raised,
cranking its throb-throb songs of Tyre and Troy
to the wind from Africa that whips the maze
and whistles news about that wax-winged boy.
It draws its strength by drawing lines of age
from neck to heel. It understands its charge.

10

From neck to heel. She understands her charge,
the prostrate worshipper on a plastic bed
where cats, geckoes, frogs, dogs, goats and insects urge
her to relax, for Hyacinthus said
that he could tame the wild. But her concern
is only that she tend the sacred tree
which grows beside the pool. She'll hear him run
to catch a frisbee in her dream; won't see
his foot as it sets down in a nest of snakes
within that same tree's root. However Great
this Mother's love, her son's required to exit
as scripted. Cut. She weeps, she curses fate.
Her anger is bright magma. From its pyre
it can hurl rocks at ships, can blaze pure fire.

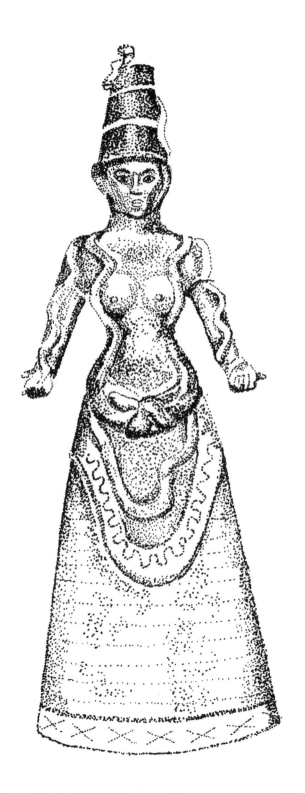

11

It can hurl rocks at ships, can blaze pure fire,
poetic imagination. Or it swims
the length of a pool and back. Locals retire,
and migrants come to land. A creed chants hymns
in the little church, but the oleanders
repeat their own psalm which says: although we're
poisonous in all parts, we welcome wanderers
from Africa, parched as you are, sit here.
The many drowned are swimming in his head
as he powers up and down. Beside him, live
mythologies are floating, playing dead
but breathing, tranquil as fresh waves arrive
and break the white from dreams. Church doors are wedged
to keep the aliens out. Gods have been purged.

12

'And keep the aliens out.' Gods have been purged
by sun from this leathern creature with a net
who catches the floating wasps, one who has forged
his own way of survival here in Crete,
whose father saw the paratroopers hacked
and joined the frenzy. No one should be meek
before a dangerous swarm. On every act
the sun gazes, gives its blessing. If a cheek
is burned, it's seldom turned. And still they land,
these dreamers who have heard of Europe, how
it grants, nurtures, restores. Reach out your hand
but leave your net behind, old man, in your slow
cleansing of the pool. Such murders make no sound.
Though here is where the first of them was found.

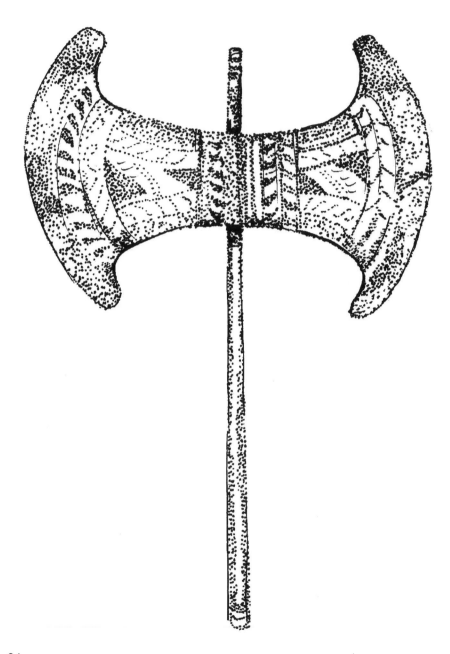

24

13

Though here is where the first of them was found,
the powers have gone from Crete, unless these wings
that swoop to snatch up what has not been drowned
were once themselves received as programmings
by faithful servers. Look at how that altar
of white blades on the mountain ridge is trying
to signal that it's true. The house lights falter,
a tripswitch goes, and soon our air-con's dying.
The flies move in; we are quite powerless.
What crashing wakes us then? Down on the floor
a thing unnatural, cut off, a feathered mess
that flew at our invisible screen door
and lies there. Not a sign of life. No sound.
A sky-god helpless on the stony ground.

14

A sky-god helpless on the stony ground
inspecting you. Exemplar of creation,
a fly-by-wire sharp style, admired, marooned:
a nation that's become a constellation,
the tail displaying twenty-eight small stars
but no sun. It is never going to leave,
caught in an endless passport queue... and where's
Ariadne to guide you home? Her love
has run off with the necessary line,
so here you are – quite lost, no bag, no phone,
on someone else's island. Yet this is fine.
Miraculously, blood drips from the stone
these words: there will be someone that you meet
(Europa on his back) who swam to Crete.

15

Europa on his back, he swam to Crete
since gods could do whatever god-lust wanted.
She had no power, she only had her fate.
His children came, yet still her childhood's haunted,
a labyrinth, a distant stifled roar:
Love, it cries, to laughter. The thread unwinds.
You've read the myths. At Pasiphaë's door
an upright, bronze, robotic figure stands
with one vein, Daedalus's secret wire,
from neck to heel. It understands its charge.
It can hurl rocks at ships, can blaze pure fire
and keep the aliens out. Gods have been purged,
though here is where the first of them was found,
a sky-god helpless on the stony ground.

Acknowledgments

Thanks to Nick Everett and Rory Waterman of New Walk Editions, to Stuart Henson and Martyn Crucefix for reading and commenting on the poems, to my family for their part in the story, and particularly to my daughter, Rosie, for providing such fine illustrations. More examples of her work can be found in my Egypt memoir *Threading a Dream: a Poet on the Nile* (Gatehouse Press, 2017) and at www.etsy.com/shop/RosalindArt.

List of Illustrations by Rosie Greening:

Cover image and on pages 9 and 27: *Europa and the Bull* – based on an Attic Red Figure vase painting (5th century BC) in the National Archaeological Museum of Tarquinia.

On page 11: *Plane Tree* – at Gortys (or Gortyna), where Europa is said to have been deposited by Zeus.

On pages 12, 14, 17, 19, 22, 25 and 29: *Labyrinth* – from the archetypal Cretan design, found especially on coins.

On pages 13 and 24: *Labrys* – sacred Minoan double axe from the Heraklion Archaeological Museum. Knossos was also known as the Labyrinth, signifying 'House of the Double Axe'.

On page 16: *Bull's Head* – based on the stone 'rhyton' (carved in black steatite) from the Palace of Knossos (1700-1450 BC), Heraklion Archaeological Museum.

On page 18: *Swallow in Flight*.

On page 21: *Great Snake Goddess* – based on the faience figurine from Knossos (1600 BC), Heraklion Archaeological Museum.

Rosie Greening is a London-based artist who specialises in faces and places. When she isn't drawing and painting, she writes children's books for a small publisher.